Dolly Mixtures

By the Pupils of

Newdigate Primary School

PRINTED & PUBLISHED BY:
The Button Press, Stafford
01785 214434
Newdigate. Primary School
February 1999
ISBN 1 84132 027 7 £4.99

Introduction

Our children can now say that they are real authors!

We are very proud of our school and of the work that the children have done to enable us to publish our own book.

Well done everyone!

Me and my Family

Me and my family

Me and my dad love playing on the computer.
Me and my mum like going shopping.
My brother lewis likes playing wiht me.
My dad takes me out anywhere. He buys me sweets.
My mum buys me clothes and shoes.
Lewis likes playing with me on his skates.

By Danielle Roberts (10years)

Me and My Family

Me and My Mum like to play on My computer.
My dad goes to work MuM plays Music.
MuM likis 70's I like 80's
I like watching telly Mum listens to radio

Mark spiers (9 yrs)

Me and my family

In my family there are four people,
Me, my brother and my mum and dad.
We go on outings quite alot
I go to school every day.
My favourite lesson is English
and I think I'll get a good education.

Emma carnell age 10

Me and My family

In my family I have two grown-ups
and me. I have got a pet gold fish.
I had two fish but one died.

Samantha Sheldon
age 9

Me and my family

Me and my family do lots of things together. We go to the park on sunny days in our swimming suits and our swimming trunks. Sometimes we play golf. And ride on the donkeys that my uncle owns. Sometimes we go on the boats.

MARy - Anne Fraser
age Nine

Me and my family

Me and my brother Sometimes play on my computer and when my brother gets involved in a programme and I go and Lose it he goes bright red and Looks Like he will explode into a thousand pieces. My Favourite person in the family is my mum because She always helps me and She is a really Special mum. Mum makes me Laugh when I feel Sad and it cheers me up.

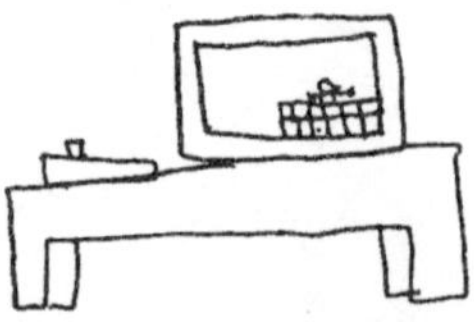

David Mills Age 9

Me and My family

I like playing with my family.
I like them playing in myroom.

Kerry Worwood

age 5

Me and my Family Laugh all the time and we have a great time. Me and my dad were Jumping up and down and my dad fell Off The bed He did not laugh but I did.

by Karl Hope age 8

Me and my family

I love my family. I have two brothers and sisters.

Steven Priest

age 5

Me and my family

My baby cousin is crazy her name is Holly May. She is very cute she has got a cute face. She often runs into the door then she runs to her mum and starts to cry. She runs after me and gives me her teddies and i run after her with them. She runs after me and gives me kisses and big hugs. We play on her baby see-saw and she laughs.

by Cherise Smith

age 8½

Me and my Family

My cousins are Called lauren and Kieran and the oldest lauren goes horse ridding She started where She Was one year old For a three year old She is quite brainy because She can count to ten it is really unusual For a three year old it is Verry old.

Kirsty Rackham Age 7

Me and my Family.

my nan sometimes helps in school, and my dad is chairman of the governers at this School. We also like pets but we dont have any. We also like boardgames, and playing cards and dominoes. Me and my sister use each other as punchbag Sometimes my sister asks me if she plays on my game boy.

year 4 Age: 8 Matthew Cairns

Me and my family

me and my family
LIRe going to
Skegness.
Jordan Teeling

Age 5

me and my family
my family members are called
the mitchells.
big Natalie and Frank
and Ron and Lesleyand gran andsam
Natalie 7
Mitchell

Me and My family

One Night My family went over to my Nans. we went out side and the moon was shining over the pond. we skidded my Brother fell in the pond. It was so funny Me and my sister laughed our heads off.

Shane Hope age 8

I love my Grandad really much. I wish I could see him soon, and his cat Whiskers.

Nicole Kincode age 4
Reception.

me and my family

I like to play with my brother on his skateboard. me and my family play dominoes too. I had a cat a dog a rabbit and a horse. I love horse riding.

I love my Mum and my dad and they love me.

Nicole Mandara
age 8

me and my family

me and my mum Dad and my sister have a good time in the summer. We go for a picnic and we take some sandwhiches and crisps. Some times we go swimming and buy clothes from town.

Natasha Frake age 7

My mum

I love my mum
my mums hoovercng
up

James Thould
Reception age 6

On Christmas Eve my Mother
read. The Story once again
Of how the little child was
born, And of the three wise
men,

And how, by following the Star
They found him where he lay
And brought him gifts and that
is why, we keep our Christmas
Day.

Damien Silvester

me and my family. my name is kristian.
I Have a dog called TAZ He is
a Bull dog. He is some Times nasty
to me and good to my sister
Everyday But to my friend he
starts Jumping up when he comes
Rond to My house But he likes him

Kristian Lecointe

Age 6 Years 2S

My family

I like my family.

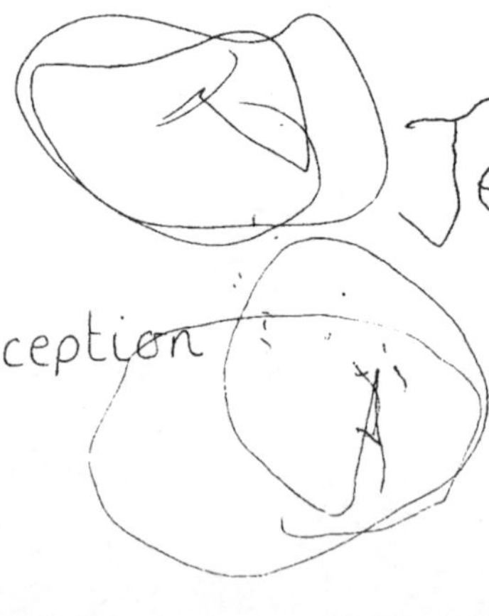

Jessica Moss

Age 4 Reception

Me And My Family.

One day me and my family went to the American Adventure Park for the day. My Mum, Dad and my self went on the Triple Log Flume. My sister did not like it so she went on the small ride when we went on the big one. Later we had something to eat and we went home. When we got home my Mum said "Did you enjoyy it?" and I said that it was wet but fun. I want to go again to that fun place.

Lewis Roberts age 11

my family

me and my family. I had a party.
I had a good time.

Charlie Abbison
age 5

My family

me and my dad go up to the

garge and work. We work

with Wood My Mum paints

What we Make.

Danial Huckridge aged 6

My Hobbies

My HOBBIES

My hobbies are art, dinosaurs, bug's and ghost's and Animals. my first hobby was dinosaurs which I started at 1. Then Animals also at 1. The ~~it was~~ art and bug's at 2 And ghost's at the age of three

Adam grovenor
age 10

My hobbies.

My favourite hobby, is going on the big Square PC because it is very interesting and it has got different programmes that I can use, like writing stories and the print Artist's. That gives me really good pictures that are very interesting. There are really brilliant games and I can find information about Romans and poor people. Computers are really good inventions.

Amanda oliver
age 8

my hobbies

My Fawourite player
is Alan shearer
becawse he kicks
The ball hard
and He is a
good Play er some
times

sam Pearson 7

My hobbies

My hobbies are football.
My hobbies are football.
I love football.
My hobbies are football.

by Danieh McArthur
Age 10

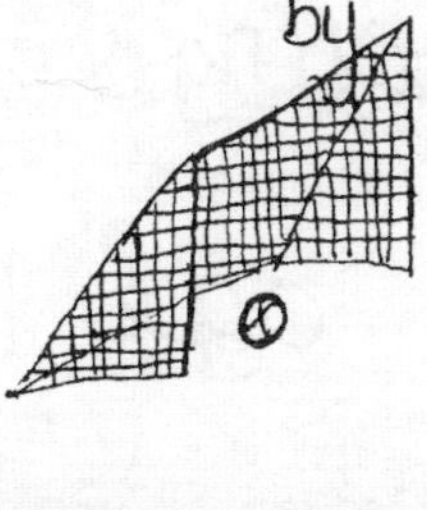

My hobbies

My hobb IS Colleting small SoLDIER toys and I've got a rcher and 12 Chip Hazzrds and I've got a drill Cycle.

Aaron Barnes 7

My hobbies

my hobbies are football, running mysteries, and army. my first hobby army began at the age of 3 and I started playing football when I was one.

By Stuart pallett age 11

My hobbies

I'm watching football its 90
Minutes long. and while its going
on im Singing man.u's Song.

I Sing it loud I Sing it proud
I love man united and So does the
crowd
but When its all over a tear
runs down my check
because man u have won And
I cant even Speack.

Lee Scott age 10

my hobbies

my FAvrite pLAyer is
fowler becuase he is
the best and Good player
becuase he is A Greatt player
and he is fantastic player
as well And he is
brilliant at soccer he is
my player For a long
time So thats why
I'm his Fan For ever

Brian Coffey AGe 8

my hobbies

my hobbie is Football and I like England. I would like to score goals like Darren Huckerby. He plays For coventry and they are my best team.

by Lewis Roberts
age 8

My Hobbies

I like running because it Keeps me healthy. I run ten times up my garden with my brother. I likes swiming Because its important incase you drown.

by Robyn Deacon
(9yrs)

Ben
Beck (10yrs)

My hobbies

My favourite hobby is football and rounders it is good fun. I like football best becuase you get to score goals and run around. I like rounders and best becuase you get energy.

My Hobbies 

my hobby is singing and dancing and looking after animals. I sing and dance to steps and bwitched. I like cats and dogs but I hate spiders I have got some at my dads house. They are dogs and cats there names are Ben, ellie and sam.

emmacoms age 7 25

my hobbies

my hobbies is basketball.

my hobbies is sleep.

my hobbles is playing with my dad

kyle Gilchrist

age 6years 2 5

My Hobbies

My hobbies are Netball which I do after school on Mondays. And my other hobbie is daancing which is realy fun. I go every Saturday its fun because as well as dancing we have partys

Eloise Connell (9yrs)

My hobby

Me and my dad love to go shooting every Sunday. We shoot rabbits and pheasants. We go to Birchcoppice near Nuneaton in Warwickshire. One week we shot 3 rabbits and 2 pheasants. We give them to my Grandad who eats them
Me and my dad like going shooting

ROSS Morris
Age 10

my Hobbies

my hobbies is art I like doing it because it is fun when get up I get a piece of paper and do some art I like drawing tree's

aged 6 Katharyn simth

My hobbies.

I helped my mum shopping and my dad. Then we went home. I played on my play station. I played Batman and Robin I was Batman. then I changed being Robin. Then I got Robins vehicle it was called Red birb

Kyle Hollyman aged 6

My hobby

My best hobby is collecting playstation games. When you first play one it gets exciting. And when you have it for two years it get boring. When I complete it I sell it and get a new one.

Kyle Beck age 9

my hobbies

Ilike drawing with my dad because he Is good at drawing. Ilike playing with him he likes to draw cars and jets

Adam aged 6

My hobby

My hobby is swimming and I go on Saturdays. It is very cold when I get in. I have lots of certifcates. My teacher is called Tina. It is lots of fun and it's very cold when I get out of the pool. My Friend Samantha goes aswell.

Rebekca Twigger Age 9

My Hobbyes

MyHobbey is PLayingWith my Freind Michael. He helps me on my Batman and RoBin game. I have Fun Playingwich my Freind Michael.

Connor aged 6

<u>My hobbeys</u>

I like to ride my bike my bike is pink.
I ride up my street.

By victoria Brownhill
aged 8.

My Hobbies

I help My Mum at work Sometimes. She works For tony She is a labourer. She build things. Tony Cutters something it is really really noisy when Tony is cutting. I help My Mum carry Somethig.

Jamie-Leigh aged 6

My hobby

My hobby is football I Play it after School all the time I Play with my friend

by Benjamin aged 8

My hobbjes

My hobbies are going to partys. We play games and we eat party food like cakes and after we have had some food we have a dance.

Shannon Kincade

age 5

My hobbeys

I like bird watching because I like to see all the different kinds.

I like golf because I want to get a hole in one

by Ben S

My hobbies

My hobby is playing with my brother. What I like doing to my brother best is tickling him.

Ashleigh Simons
Age 5

<u>My Hobby</u>

when I run down the pitch I score a goal. When I am on the pitch I think I am Andy cole and I score another goal.

By Christopher Glass

aged 8.

My hobby

My. hobby is playing with my sewing. I use a big fat needle and when I push the needle through the material it make's a bigger hole than it's supposed to. And the thread wont go in the hole in the needle. I'm sewing a picture of a duck. My nan gave me it for christmas.

age 8 Amy Ryan

My hobbies

I like to play football. My favourite football team is Newcastle.

Reeca Stafford

age 5

My hobbies

I like to build things with my grandad. we have fun.

James Lee

age 5

My Hobby is cycling because I can sandwich my brother between the kerb and me and anoy him. I scrape his tyre and he calls me stupid. I also like it because it keep's me fit and healtty. I hope whe I grow up I can be a bike racer.

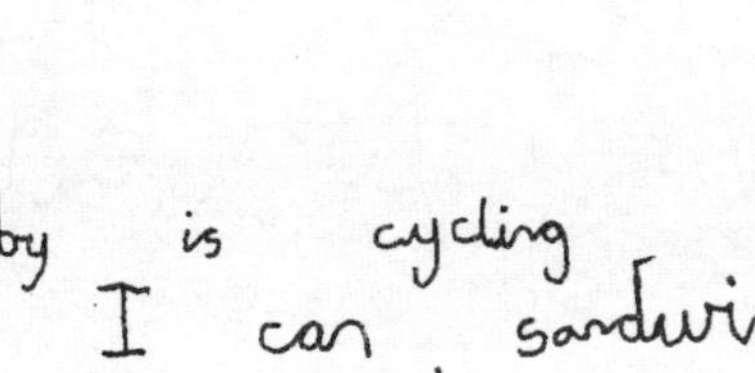

Phillip Grace
age 8

My hobbies

I like playing with my dad. I love my dad. I love playing hide and seek

Bleau Towland
age 5

I love football I like Manchester United best
Thomas Whitehead age 5

My hobbies

I go swimming I have a special swimming costume I can go under the water when I get goggles

Chelsee

Chelsee McKinlay

Age 5 Reception

My hobbies

I like swimming I go with my Mum I like going in the water

elleen

ch>

chantelle walkinshaw

Age 4 Reception

My Hobbies

My hobbies are football being as active as I can, scoring loads of goals and doing terrific Saves. I Will Score from the half Way line, and bury a penalty dribbling round the players till foul!!!

John Shotton (10)

My Hobby

My hobby is football because it is active, you can score great goals and win dramatic penalties, smack a free kick in the back of the net and watch the goalie pick it out. I dribble the ball round the defenders, the keeper comes out, I chip it, it goes up over the goalie! It dips! Goal!!!

Andrew McKenzie age 11

My Hobbies

My Hobbies are Swimming and football.

I like Swimming because it is fun.

I like football because it is sporty.

I swim at Bedworth Baths with Bobi and Katie.

I like football because I play with Nathan and some of his friends

Jenny Dee Age 10

Favourites at School

I like literacy Hour because it is good.
I like doing Wellington square with Mrs Steel we use a C.D Rom.

by susan oliver

My favourite things about School is Story Writing because every time we do Story writing I have ideas buzzing all around my head Like bumble bees. I can do lots of pages in my story book. I like Writing adventure Stories and I Like it When my teacher reads my Story to the class.

by Calley Mc Arthur
Age 9.

My favourite things about school

I Like Literacy hour because we have a big book and we read it with Our teacher and we talk about the big book and then we go and do some work about the words in it. age 8

by Sophie moffat

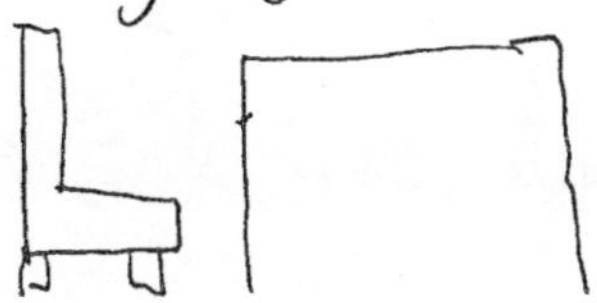

My favourite things about school

I love to paint
When I showed the teacher she nearly fainted.
I love to draw
But my picture nearly brock the law.
I love to lean
When somone's naughty everybody turns.

Abbie Davies (9 yrs)

My Favourite things about School

I like Art and Painting and chalking and reading BooksI love School I like Boing Art all the time It is very nice at School I like at School it is nice

Katie Fenn age 7 years 2S

Vanessa Dykes (9years)

My favourite things about School.

My favourite things are maths, I like maths because I like adding, and Time's Tables. Mostly I like adding because they are So easy, and I Sometimes I like history because you can get in to it. When it's play time I don't really want to stop literacy Hour. I like literacy Hour because it changes every time, like one day it's hard the next day it's really easy. I like P.E. Some times, because we some times get the apparatus out. What I like most about this School is the Head teacher mis Waterfield I like her very much.

my favorite things about school

My favorite things about school is Handwriting and maths and writing and I like Hometime becouse I like going Home

RHYS Armstrong Age 7

My favourite subjects at school.

My favourite subject is creative writing. We write extremely long stories, Mrs Waterfield teaches us, she helps alot.
We use lots of brilliant words like, fabulous, terrifying, and brilliant. My favourite story I wrote was how the squirrel became. Another of my favourite subjects is Geography. We are doing India. We had to write down everything we know and I didn't know alot.

Gemma Cleveley (10)

My favorute things about school

when I walk to school in the morning all by myself and when we do maths and P.E; all other stuff. The best thing that, I like R.E and we have dinner and go out to play and do work and when the bell goes we get ready and go home.

by
sarah
white
age 9

my favourite. things about school are doing P.E on friday. I like handwriting when we do it. I like painting a picture for my mummy.

Fiona Thomson
age – 7 years

My favourite things about school

At school I like to do maths. At school I like to do writing and colouring. At school I like to do art. At school I like to read Books. At school I like to draw pictures. At school I like to count.

Nicole wiggan age - 6 years 25

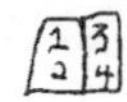

Katie Earl. (10 yrs)

My Favourite Things About School.

My favourite things about School are that you do p.e and games.
I like my teacher,
And I like all my friends,
because I have lots of people to play with.

My favourite thing about School.
I like everybody at School. We play wich paint. My teacher is mr Johnson he is a man teacher We are all very helpful to mr Johnson.

Charlotte Evans
aged 6.

My Favourite Things About School.

My favourite things about school are when the teachers give you merit points for doing good work. I like doing P.E. especially apparatus.
I absolutely love doing maths because I will get a good education.

By Penny Hodgson (Class 5 E)

age 10

My favourite thung about school.

I like doing paniting at school. I like playing with the toys. I like reading in school. My teacher is mr Johnson and he's nice. I like everybody at school. I lick Paige, Charlotte, Chelsee, Leigh and Katheryn.

Rebecca wilson aged 6

My favourite things about school

My favourite things about school are play times because you get to play football. I like maths and history, especially Egyptians and Romans.

Kenny Smith

age 9

My Favourite things about School.

I love Maths because I am good at it.

Art is good fun.
P.E especially playing games

Martin Hill aged 9.

my Favourite thing about school.

I like school because it is
Fun.
I enjoy writing.

Ryan blase aged 6

My favowrite thing a bowt schoolis working.

Shannon Beck
Age 5

My favourite things about School

My favourite things about school are Art, playing, Maths, p.E, my teacher and merit ports. I like them all because you get a good education and the best thing about school is your teacher and your friend.

Sarah Deacon
age 9 (class 5E)

My favourite thing at school.

My favourite thing at school is Maths because I can answer every question I am given to do.

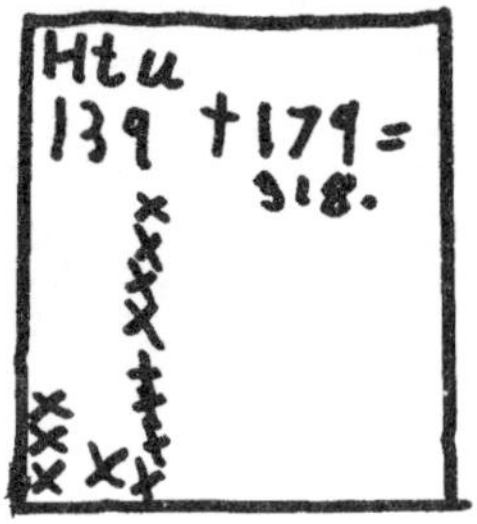

by Jennifer. Aged 9.

I likeplaying inthe playground. I like hopskotch.

Karla Fitzpatrick age 4

reception

At school I love playing with the remote control car at school.

Ideta James age 4
Reception

My favourite things at school

My favourtie thing at school is literacy hour because we can Share a big book and We ask questions and at the end of the Week We write about the book; its called a book review and at the end of literacy hour we have a plenary session When we discuss the the book and talk about What weve learned

Corinne Jellis Age 7

My favourite things at school

I like playing with money at school I like the playdough because we make stuff with it Jessica Shortall

Age 4 Reception

My favourite things at school

I like drawing and playing.
I like listening to Mrs Carlas stories.

Cherise Johnson

Age 4 Reception

My Favourite Things about School

I enjoy maths, science, R.E., games, art, geography and D.T., I don't like English. I enjoy it when it's a wet play time because I don't like being in the freezing cold. I like all of the teachers, but I like Mr. Grimley because he is a wicked games teacher. I like maths and we interact with the equipment.

Daniel White age 11

My favourite things about school.

I like having the toys
I like doing jigsaws
I like writing perryHBPR

Age 4 Reception

Heroes and Heroines

The

HEROS.

My hero's big and Strong. Hes 50 X what I am and thats why he's my hero. His name is Schwarznegger, Arnold Schwarznegger. He Stars in lots of movies.

I have another hero. Hes called John claude Van damme. He looks quite nice. BY Kelly-Ann Mandaea
10 Years old.

Heroes and heorines

My Hero is Superman. He is a strong man. He can lift a car-

Aaron Bredges
Age 5

Heroes and Heroines

My hero is my dad because He is strong.

Christopher carter
Age 5

I Wish

I wish I was a football player I wish I player for Brazil to play with Ronaldo. Me and Ronaldo at Front to score lots of goals and be the best goal scorer in the World. And take penalties.

By Daniel Ward (9 year old)

natalie walkinshaw
(10yrs

Heroes + Heaines.

My hero is my dad.
In the super market I got lost,
my dad saved me because he found me.
I love my dad,
He is the best dad in the world.
In the shopping centre I fall and I
couldn't walk at all, and guess who
saved me? my dad!

by natalie walkinshaw
(10yrs)

Heroes and heroines

My sister is my heroine
because she saved my
life when I fell in
the bath.

Luke Ryan.
age 5

I am a hero batman

I rescue people from danger

Max Wilson age 4

Reception

Heroes + Heroines

My heroine is my mum. She should be called the one and only super mum. Shes like my wings, the star in the sky. She cooks for me, cleans for me and tucks me in at night. To me shes like a rose all on her own.

By Lauren Morgon Payne (10 years.)

My hero

I would like to be like Spiderman and do some cobwebs because he is great and I watch him o TV

Ieuan

e

Ieuan Lewis

Ag 5 Reception

My hero

My hero is Noel Whelan who plays for Coventry City Football Club. The only reason he is my hero is because he Scores lots of goals For Coventry. I watch Noel Whelan Some times in High Field Road.

Daniel Glass

age 10

My hero

My hero is Alan Shearer who plays for England He Scores Lots of goals. When England is on T.V I watch it. Alan shearer is the best.

Jonathan Hammond
age 10

My hero

I want to be like Dipsy because he is good He hides from everyone

W a p(1)

Wade Huscroft

Age 6 Reception

My hero

I want to be like spider-man because he is real ife chases people and catches [illegible] Lewis

Lewis Hope

age 5 Reception

<u>My heroes.</u>

<u>Jason Mandara age 10.</u>

My heroes are Andy cole and Dwight York of Manchester United. Man U is my favourite team. I think they're the best. Andy cole and Dwight York is my heroes because they're are always scoring minute after minute. They zoom here and zoom there. They work as a team - a superb team. I watch Man U on the T.V and I like it when they score because the fans get up and cheer and the other team shouts boo
I like it when they say boo because they get jealous.

and

My hera bea acause he iz strog
I want to
will beat my dad He has
got a parther Batmen

Matthew

Age 5 Reception

Matthew Challenger.

My hero is Gary Lineker because he scoresall the goals. He never fouls other players and he can tackle other players really well. I want to bea footballer because I'm a good footballer now but I need to do lots of training first.

by Thomas Turnbull age 7

My hero is Cantona because he scored lots of goals. He some times got a red card because he was good at headers. Cantona used to be in Man-u. I wish I could be a football player when I grow up I can train at football training. We have a club at school to practice football I'm going to join this.

Name: Cade Richardson age: 9

Heroes And Heroines

Your heroes can be anyone, Football players singers even ordinary people.

Just think, Firefighters, police, ambulance people they save people every day.

Just think of all of the heroes and heroines in the world.

My Favourite hero is Dwight Yorke, he is a football player who plays for Manchester United.

Ian Patel 11

Heroes and Heroines

When we think of heroes we tend to think of super-type characters. The real heroes are police firefighters and ambulance people but heroes are also ordinary people who do brave things. Jack is one of these heroes. One night while picking up a lady in his ambulance, the doctor became ill and he was left with a pregnant woman about to give birth. Luckily for the lady, Jack was studying to be a doctor so, with a lot of effort Jack pulled her through it and was hailed a hero.

James. Freeman Age 11

My hero is Ryan Giggs because he scores every single time he plays a match. Ryan Giggs never gets a red card because he never fouls. He skids across field and he scores, He kicks the ball to the other side and he scores again. Nobody can be as that football player because he trains every day. But I'm joining the football club so I might be as good as him when I grow.

by Phillip Clee age 9

my hero

My hero is Russell. He held my bike I did not fall in the bushes.

Owen Hopkins
age 6

My Hero

My hero is Batman. BATMAN fights Mr. Freeze.

Ryan Malpass aged 6

Heros and Heroines

My dad is my hero and. he's like Batman and he's strong like Superman. And he's better than all the rest. He's even Better than the dog at Raceing

Daniel challenger age 7

My Heros

One day I Slipped on the muddy water and batman saw me in the water. He was my Heroes. I went to his house and I Stayd there for ever. I will be rescuing people. we will be happy.

Brian millar

7

Heroes and Heroines.

My Hero is My DaD and his other KiD. One day I nearly Fell off a cliff But he saveD me. I tripped over and he caught me Before I fell in the river. I saved him once When he didn't see a rock and fell into the river But I got his hand Before he fell in. By Ben Muscroft Age 7

Heroes and Heroines. 

my hero is Beckham He plays for man united and sports England. Beckham is the Best player of the foot ball player He was all ways playing foot ball when it was foot ball time and a man got the ball off him.

Jack cant age 7 years 2s.

My Hero

is my Dad can lift a heavy box with his tools in He mends things in our house.

Paul McKee Age 6

Heroes and Heroines

my hero is Daniel. He saved my cousin called Jack from getting run over a car came through the gates and Jack neary ran in front of the car and Daniel grabbed his coat

Kellie Bingham age 7 years

Heroes and Heroines

my Hero is terminator. He rides a motrbike and he is a robot. He does not look like a terminator. He looks like a man.

Shane Green Age 8

Pets

My Pet

my pet is a guinea pig.
His name is casper.
He likes to lick my finger.
And run around his cage.
His favourite food is cucumber
And cabbage, carrots and apples.
by simon Argyle age 11

My pet

My hamster knocks down his drink. It hides food and it digs under wood scrapings and it tears things. When he gets out he runs fast. We have to dash after him. He never plays with his wheel. He gets his food in a mess. His name is Tom.

by daniel clewley age 7.

'my Pet

one day I let my Pet Snake out for food. He chased a mouse and rats. Healways comes back and I always give him a big rat. When he is fast a sleep I pick him up and put him by the window so he will get strong.

David Sheldon age 7

My Pet Hamster

My hamster is as white as a snowball.
And he runs around in a yellow fun ball.
He eats his bedding.
Which also does his head in.

By Duane Hodgson, aged 11

I WISH

I WISh I could play Golf LIKe TIger Woods. I WISh I could have golf Lessons off TIger Woods

By Luke HORton

age 10

my Pets

my pets are a dog and a puppy and two cats I Love my Pets and my Pets Love me.

Jade Longmuir

age 5

My pet.

My pet is a Spotted white rabbit She nips and bites alot. She eats rabbit food, carrots, cheddar biscuits and sleeps in the vegetable shed or her hutch and runs away from everyone. Chantelle Jefferson Age 11

my pet

I love my pet He is a hamster His name is hammy it is a boy. He etes sand whiches and sizzling sausages. He is use to me and he is not use to anyone else. He is 6 weeks old

age 8 michelle donnelly class 3a

my pet

we looked after my name parrot and it madea squailing noise. It gave me a headache.

by snone Freeman

7

My Pet

Jack is my pet dog,
He's a Jack Russell bread,
He loves his Pedigree Chum
He is very lazy,
And sleeps alot,
But I love him to bits,
Because he's my dog.

By Ryan McCartney
Aged 11

My Nana's pet

My Nana's dog is called Bussbie. And he enjoys playing with his bouncy ball. Plus he likes going on Long walks. And the colour of his fur is cream and white. He is two years of age. At night time Bussbie sleeps by the single bed on his own. When he sleeps through the day he sleeps by the fire.

Carl Mitchell
AGE 10

My pets

I have a cat called rose she likes eating Food, her Favourite is beef. She Chases Mice and rabits, she Likes wool and string.

Chloe. McILWraith age 7

MY Dog

The one who listens when I talk.
The one who cheers my lonley walk.
The one who nuzzles when I sigh.
The one who comfort when I cry.
Who else but
You.... MY loving dog.

by Karl
Walsh
age 10

My pet

My pet is a black and white
rabbit called Barney
Who runs around in his cage
At night he sleeps in his bed bit
With a Jumper.
He harmless and playful to everyone
by Justine Moss Age 10

My pet

My pet was the best pet ever because he used to sing "Dixie" and Whistle alot. He was green and gellow and his hair stook up. His name was Billy.
. He was quiet at night, but loud in the morning. Two weeks after my Birthday he flegaway. I WISh he Would come back.

By
Lance Fawcett age 10

my Pet

my Pet dog sleeps in a basket by the wall and the table. She is called Bambi and is a small dog. She's very old but she sometimes bites.

Tanya varnam age 8.

My pet

I have two gerblies and they are the best pets I ever had. Their names are bubble and squeak. They like me taking them out of their cage. They like running on the sofa and they like me cuddling them.

Kirsty Marshall. age 7. 25.

My Pet

My pet is a budgie he is called Georgie if there is any music on he will dance like moving from side to side and he will Jump up and down when he comes out he alway goes to my mum and won't come to me or my brother. When my mum is not in the room he comes out and he follows us everywhere even up the stairs to our rooms. Georgie dosen't talk but he can ring like the telephone and when we have vistors. They think its the real phone and wonder why we don't answer it.

Kerry Chamley (9yrs)

my pet

my pet is a dog her name is rosie. I take her for a walk. I give her treats She is a black and white border collie

Laura Benn 2'S 7

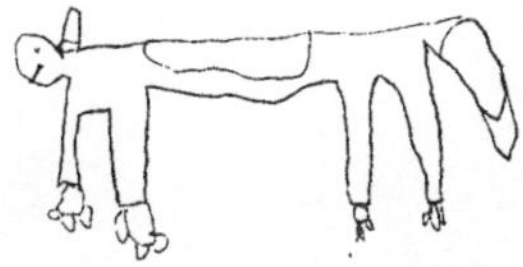

My Pet

My pet is a hamster named Joe, he is brown and white. If you hold him he crawls on you. If you give him some food he will stay there and ask for more, When you clean him out he carefully climbs into the ball. He rolls around in his ball untill he bangs into somethings.

By Kimberley Sturdy (age 9)

My Pet

My pet is my bird named Ferdie. He always comes and tries to eat my dinner and he likes salt and pepper. He sometimes climb's on my shoulder and nibbles your hair all the time

Liam Jefferson age 7 2S

My pet Jennifer (9Yrs) taylor

My kitten's name is Tod, he keeps trying to get the birds and the fish that live in our house. Graene keeps taking him of me, and won't let me fuss him. If I'm naughty then I have to say bye bye to him. I hope he'll never die. Although I spoil him he never stay on my lap. The only time he stays on my lap is when he is sleepy or too busy biting and scratching me. He's least favourite place is the laundry basket (it is a prison when he is naughty.)

My pet

My Mum said to my Dad their is something in the bedroom. My Dad said no there is not, Go back to sleep. My Mum went to the toilet. when my Mum came back my Dad went too. My Dad saw something scurrying across the landing. when my Dad turned the light on it was my hamster Rosa.

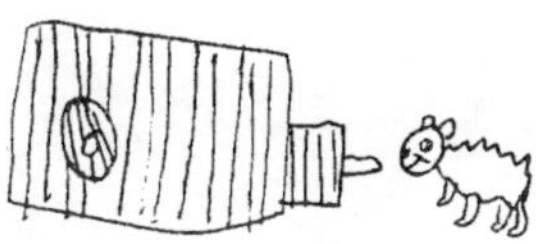

Hannah Bridges 2S

Age 6

My pet

My pet is a beautiful pet called Robbie the rat. He is really friendly. Only, if you squeeze his belly he will bite but he is a lovely pet he is my friend. He goes mad for a treat.

By Keisha McDonald (9yrs)

My pet

My pet is Hoppy. He bites my moms finger Hoppy loves to eat carrots I have got 2 dogs at home. Their names are Bess and sindy.

Laura McPheat age 7

My pet

My pet is a dog.
My pet loves playing ball.
My pet is a fuss pot.
My pet does anything for food.
My pet is a girl.
My pet sleeps in a basket.
My pet barks at the door when someone is there.

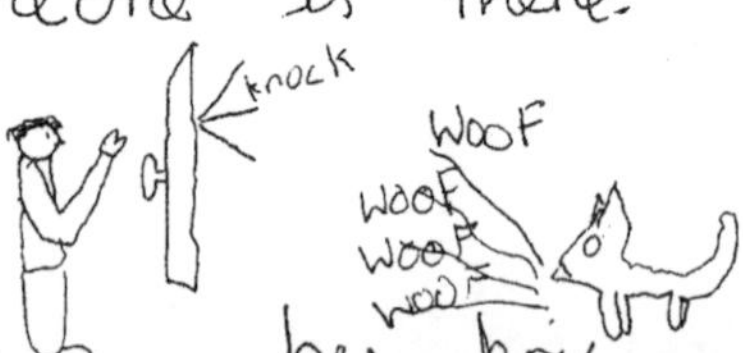

by kris varnam (9yrs)

my pet

my pet is funny. It chases his tail and it bites my feet. my dogs name is kim and it is called a bitch.

Daniel mitckhell

age 6 years

2S

My pet.

My pet is a bird named Cookie.
I like to teach it to Sing a Song by Whisting.
Sometimes I tell it to Shut up because it gets on my nerves.
It's really cute because it whistle's it's Self to Sleep.
It used to lay eggs but they always died

By Abigail Turnbull (9 yrs)

My pet.

My pet is a rabbit and his name is snowy and I Will show you snowy one day. I had snowy and we put my rabbin on the grass and my rabbit Went through a fence the next day I saw snowy and I gave snowy a bath.

John Noble

Age 6 years 2s

My Pet

My cat Mel She's mad. She runs around the room. When I go to bed Mel comes up stairs and sleeps With me and When I wake up she mieous at me. If I shut her out of my bedroom she cries so my dad comes up stairs and lets her in.

Natalie Hollyman age 10

My pet

My dog is a Maniac because on Tuesday my dog went in the garden and I Chased him. He runs around the Shed and he goes in For a drink of water.

Kirsty McDonnell
Age 10

My Pet

My Pet is a Pest. She is a Catand She is black. Her name is Twinkle. I have got 3 cats, one is Called Smokey, the other is Called Ginger

Alex Gibson
age - 7 years

My pet

My pet is a dog. It is a girl and her name is Jake. She is black and white and she likes to play with me. My dog likes to eat alot of food.

Lauren Hope Age 9

My pet

My pet is Fast She hid behind the bed and did not come out She is a girl and she is Scared when I go near her.

Rebecca Carnell Age 7 25

my pet

my pet is a little mut because she never stops playing with me I Dont mind if she jumps on the couch and chairs. She is Just a puppy. I got her before my birthday.

Demi Frew. Age 7 2S

My pet

My rabbit is a boy and its name is Thumper. When we feed him he spill it everywhere and when I clean him out he messes it up again. When we let him out to run in the garden we can't get him back in again so we have to pick him up and he bites us.

Emily Mckee age 10

My pet.

my pet is a cat,

his name is smokey.
his nice and cuddiy
he was a pest and my mum gave him away

by

Alex aged 8.

My Pets

I have a bird and a cat.

My bird is called Smoky.

My cat is called Buzz.

Leigh aged 5

My pet
My hamster lives in a cage.
I take it upstairs.
I play with it in my bedroom.

Daniel aged 6

my pet
My dog's name is Scruffy He is a boy. He is three year's old and HE is blond and fluffy

by Clare S

Age 8

My Pets.

I have ten fish in a tank. I have a cat that scratches me. The cat is called Scoobby.

Chelsee Hollihead aged 6

My Pet

I bouht a dog in april she is 1 year old. She plays with you. She bites your ears and likes jumping on you she is playful. Kim likes to go for a walk and she loves going to bed with you. She is black and brown. and when you say walk her big ears go up.

By Carl Mitchell

My pet

Once I had a rabbit. It was my very first rabbit. I loved it to bit's. Then it got all tangled up with it's fur. Me and my dad could do nothing about it. Two week's later it died

By Daniel Derricott age 8

My Pet

My Pet crept up the stairs and he got on the radiator. My Mum shouted to My Dad. My Dad put my pet back down stairs.

Jonathan sturdy aged

my pet

my pet likes balls to play with.
He likes to play in the bedroom.

Sundeep Cehai

age 6

My pet

I have two rabbits they are a Mother and daughter. They both live in the Same hutch. rabbits ned a lot of writer and food for a testy treat they have carrots leaves and even chocolate drops for babbits. Summer is there favourite time they have a run so they Stay out all day lying in the Sunshine and eating grass. my rabbits are black and ther names are lucky and chocolate Chip I love them very much. In the Winter they Snuggle up to eachother to keep warm. In the Spring I pick dandelions for them. Their hutch has got two Sides One has Sawdust in the other hay.

by Hannah Garner age 8

My pet

My pet is a cat her name is Sophie. She is a playful cat.

by Victoria Owens
Age 8

My Pet

I love my dog. I cuddle it.

Jolee Derbyshire
age 5

My pet

My pet is a budgie, and her name is flow, and it's a girl but she bites, she chews paper and evry time you try and write she will chase your pen

by: sarah manolby

Age: 8

My pet.

I have a big dog.
It is black and grey.

Donovan Lessey.

Age 5

My pet

My pet is called Candy.
She is a dog.
She likes dog food.

Craig Mejia
age 5

My pets.

I have got five pets, three at my house and two at my dads. I have got a dog called Sindy, a rabbit called Lola and a kitten called Rosey at my house and two dogs called Bruce and Franlin at my dads house. Bruce is a huge ridge back and Franklin is a little staffie. The funny thing is Bruce is the biggest and Franklin is the smallest, but Bruce is younger than Franklin!! I got Rosey in 1998, Sindy in 1994 and Lola in 1997.

by Charley Nicolle Mosey

age: 8.

My Pet

My dogs name is Jade
and she is a girl and she
likes me. She plays with me.

by Laura c

4J 8.

I went to see my
rabbits. They are called
chocolate chip and lucky

Chloe Gamerage 5.

my pet

scooby is a very fluffy cat. He Likes to play attack the toy. He also Likes his warm nap by the fire and he plays alot.

by kirsty Argyle aged 8

I have 3 dogs
I like Bess she's huge

JAMIE READING

age 5

My pet

My Dog always goes crazy and she gets the food on the carpet and she licks it up and I also take her for walks Her name is Jade and she is black and brown.

sean coleman age 7

I played with my guinea pig in the house

Leah Paxton
age 5 RecBA on

My dog knocks drinks down off the chairarm. My dog sits on my bed. Sometimes he drags his dog food into the frontroom and spills it on the carpet. Mum has to clean it up.

My dogs name is Max.

KiERian Lycett age 8

MYcats

MY cats got stuck under the fire. MY cats like to play

Nathan Mckee

age 5 Reception

I have got a dog and a cat I've got a kitten and I've got another cat I've got three cats

Alyshea Ingram age 4 reception.

My Pet

my cat ginger sleeps on my bed and when ever I get into my bed he is soft and cuddly some times she scratches me and bites but she is only playing she sometimes goes to the fish bowl and licks the water. I hope he doesnt' swallow the fish.

By Stacey Morris
Age 8

my pets
my pets are really rea
reallymypetsavounite They are
fish I've
got specialxddd gor them
zoe keers

Age 5 reception

Zoe Keers

My pets
I have got a bird. We let
him out but my Mum
doesnt want him out
becouse he doent go
back
Damien

Age 5 Reception
Damien Hackleton

My Pet.

My hamster zooms around its cage, it nibbles at the metal bars. My hamster is brown and white, it has very thin fur. It eats all his food, and now he's getting fat. It's two years old, it's name is Joe, my hamster has black eyes, they look like little black beads. I never handle my cute hamster. My Dad puts him in the plastic, white ball, he flies around the cosy lounge.

Andrea Sturdy. 11

My Pet

I have a dog. He is called Nip. Nip is good. He eats his toys LEANNE

Leanne Redpath
Age 6 Reception

My Pet

My pet is a dog and his name is called Ben. And he is eight years old and he is a playful dog. He is a big black and white dog. I take him walks with my Dad and he pulls on the lead alot.

Robert Glass 10

My Pets

My pets are a dog and a cat, they are called Simba and Bambi. Simba is a creamy coloured dog and Bambi is a ginger. Simba is quite big now, he was smaller than the cat when we first got him. He barks at everyone and the cat miaows. Bambi comes and sits with you on your lap, and Simba tries to get on the chair but he's to big. So he lies under your feet instead.

Carley Magdee 11

I Wish

I wish

I wish I could play for Newcastle and beat Alun Shearers goal scoring record.

by Nathan Allison

aged 10

I wish

I wish that I was on a donkey at the beach in Blackpool.

Jade Morgan

age 5

I Wish

I wish I had a limousine
Which was white as cream
And if I had a limousine that would be
my dream

by

Keith coleman 6G 10 years

I wish

I wish my hamster
was still alive

Katie Benn

Age 5

I Wish.

I wish I could fly up to the
moon,
And float back down in
a hot air balloon,
I wish I could own all
the sweet shops,
Candysticks, lollipops.
I wish I could zoom across
the sea faster than a bumble-
bee.
So now you know what
I like to do I WISH,
I WISH, I WISH.

Shaun Jefferson
age - 11.

I WISH

I WISH I had all of
the action men in the
world.

Ashley Anderson
age 5

I wish

I wish I hed Lots of moneyso I could buy a train set.

Lewis Carlill
Age 5

I Wish

I wish you could have holidays in space. You would have lots of fun. You could swim in the milky way. I also wish you could be inside a Computer and play games. You could be Mario or Spyro the dragon, it, would be cool.

I wish! Natalie Silverwood age 11.

I wish

I wish I had a fish to float in my tank.

Sven owens

Age 5.

I Wish

I wish I could play football for England and Newcastle united. That would be my dream come true.

By Kevin Smith
Aged 11

I wish

I wish my dog was Still aLive
and I wish we didn't have an old
car and I wish we had a new
car.

James
Connell
age 5

I wish

I wish I had a dog that I could
take for a walk. and I give him
a bath and I will call her
Sally She will dig up the garden.

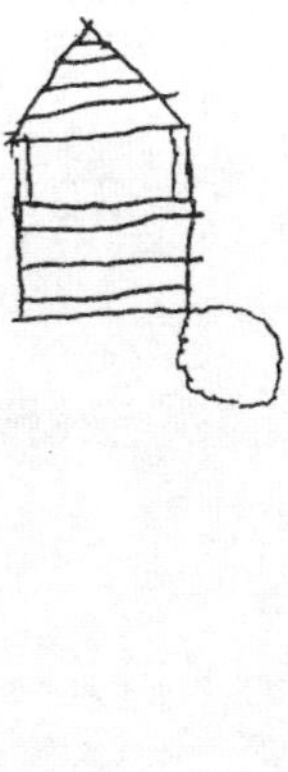

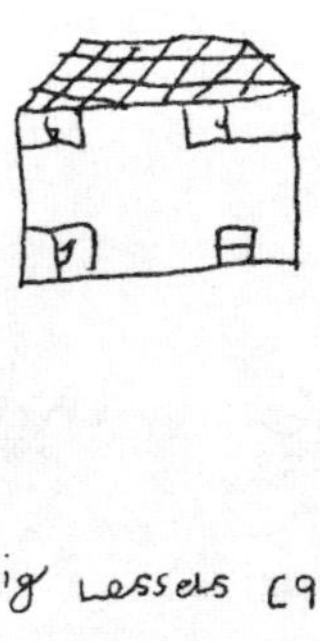

Craig Lessels (9 yrs)

I Wish

I wish I had a magic watch so I could stop time. I would never be late for school!.
I wish I had a spaceship so I could fly around. I'd be able to see if aliens are real!.
I wish I didnt have to come to school.
I think I'd never be bored!.
I wish I had a magic wand so I could do magic. I would earn money for doing tricks!.

I Wish all these wishes would come true

Michael Thould 5C (Aged 10)

I wish

I wish I could eat fish and chips

Zoe Addison
age 5

I Wish

I Wish I could fly like a bird.
Up above the Sky I'd fly,
over to Scotland and the to poland
I'd go over the wood into the forest,
then back home safe and sound

Natalie Wilson age 9

I am a space man.
I go in a rocket.
Jordan Edgar.

age 4

I Wish

I wish I was a super star,
flying high in the blue sky.
I wish I was a famous singer,
Baby, Sporty, Ginger, Posh.

I wish I was on Tv,
maybe on citv.
I wish I was an angel,
with a golden ring around my head

by claire Roso
Age 9

I wish I had a
watch I wish it was
a Barbie watch.

Lauren Lessels age 4

reception

I wish

I wish I was a fairy so I could have wings.
I wish I could fly so I can fly in the sky.
I wish I was a canary so I can sing songs.
I wish I was Cinderella so I can kiss a prince.
I wish I was a toy so I see more children.
I wish I was a Baby so I could have more time
alone with my mum.
I wish I was a book so people could read
me.

Kerrie Lynn
Age 9

I wish.

I wish I had a
big fire engine
to drive.

Jack Longmuir
Reception. Age 4

My wish

I wish my mum would let me Play Soccker and hokey I wish I could See David Backham.

by Stacey w age 8.

I wish

I wish I could be a Queen with lots of jewellery and rings and nice clothes

EMMa McKenzie

Age 4. Reception

I wlsh

I wlsh I was Batman
because I could save
everyone I like his
caper I want one Daniel

Daniel
Feast

Age 5 Receptcon

<u>My wish</u>

I wish I won the Lotterey. I would buy a new house. a car and a motor bike I would have a swimming pool in the pach and I could buy a dog.

by Richard
Silverwood aged 8

I wish

I wish I was an angel
because they fly and they
are nice to people because
they help people Siobhan

Siobhan Naismith

Age 4 Reception

I wish

I wish I could play football with
coventry city football club. I wish I
could do anything I want. I also wish
I could spend an hour with my dad's
mum and dad.

by Paul Burke aged 9

I wish

I wish I could be Barbie

because is nice and I
want to dance like Barbie

Zoe Harrison

Age 5 Reception

I am going to write about
I wish.

I wish that I could meet
micheal owen becuse he is
brilliant for England. And
I like him.

by samantha Age 8.

I Wish . . .

I wish my grandad would come back to life, life I just had a minutie with him it would make my life worth living.
I wish I could keep all the puppies that are going to be sold.
I wish that I could ride on a beutifull white mare through the shallow sea. But my greatest wish of all is that nobody in the whole wide world would never die.

by Lisa Claridge age 9

I Wish

One day I was thinking about what I wished for, "Mum why can't there be alot more swimming pools and why can't there be a lot more pet shops?" But then when I really thought carefully, I said "Mum, do you know what I wish for the most? I wish everyone was loving and caring.

Sarah Carnell 11

I Wish

I wish that I could play Cricket for England squad.
I wish that I could be rich.
I wish I can be a Knight of the round table.
I wish I could make a Origami city.
I wish that the world was not polluted.
I wish there is a end of all wars.

'I WISH!'

Michael Hill, 11½

I Wish I Wish

I Wish I could spend a few hours with my Granddad Who died in 1966.
I Wish I could have a king charles spaniel.
I Wish my parents could win the lottery.

By Laura Murphy age 9

I Wish!

I Wish that the World Was not a sad place, but a nice and happy place. Not Like having tree's chopped down and animals Losing their homes. There will be no Fields, tall tree's Will be Losing there trunk's. But no it is not Like that. I Wish!

BY Natalie Harrison age 8

I Wish

I wish that my Mum and Dad were rich and had a limousine, and a swimming pool in a big house. I wish that we all had abig room each, one for me, my brother, my sister and one big room for my Mum and Dad. I wish we all had a King size bed and a play area for me, my brother and my sister.

Bobi Gowland 10 Age

I Wish

- to be my dad because he is very intelligent.
- to be an R.S.P.C.A officer because I would be able to work wish animals such as birds, tabby cats and alsations.
- to be a Dolphin because they are very intelligent animals.

Brian sanderson age 10.

My wish

I wish that I could meet Micheal owen.
I wish he had got me a pet.
I had a dog But he died.
I wish he was alive.

by EMMA
McEwan
Age 8

I wish.

I wish I was a Football player I Love Liverpool and I wish I shot 8 times and it would be goals. I wish I had a Football video of 1999 I Love it so mush.

by christopher smith

class 4J.

I Wish

I Wish I Was a big coloured butterfly flying by the Scented flowers. I could see what's going on all day. I Wish I was a queen with glittering Jewels all around me. I'd be sitting on the trone, I'd go to big posh balls and meet the Duke of York.

Hannah Marshall 10

I wish

I wish that I could be amillionare so that I could buy myself Loads of Ice-cream because they are really yummy. I also wish for Loads of pop music like steps so I could dance to the songs. If I really was amillion-are I will beable to buy myself my own pop group. I would call it Danielles dancers.

8 years old Danielle Harrison

I wish

one Day I wish to be a Millionaire because my sister keeps tormenting me as she has more pocket money than me. If I was a millionaire I would share it with my Grandma and Grandad and I would be able to go any where.

Shane Sillverwood

Age 10

I Wish

I wish I was a footballer playing for a team. I wish I had cool ball control and was very skilful. I Wish that kevin was on my team, scoring wicked goals while I set them up what a GOAL!!!

James Gray
10

I wish

I wish the world was made out of chocolate and the floor made out of icing sugar so I could go iceskating on it. I would eat a chunk a day. The next time you saw me all you would see would be someone looking like a big fat marshmallow.

Jade mandara Age 9

I Wish

I Wish that I lived on a Island With coconuts on and I could meet David Beckham So I could Score a goal With him When he is on holiday. But you never know, I might have to use a coconut for a football. Living on a IsLand Would be the Best thing in the world especially all the coconuts.

Tina Patel Age 8

I Wish

I wish I could be a muscle man the Strongest in the world. I wish I could be a Zoologist Studying extra-ordinary creatures. I wish I could be a deep sea diver plunging into crystal clear waters.

David Grace (10)

I Wish

When I grow up I wish I could be a teacher. because I like the Sublects We do at School and I like talking. I would also be able to Learn lots of New things all the time.

by Emma Taylor Age 8

I wish

- to be superman and save troubled people.
- to be a fireman and help alley-Cats who are stuck up trees.
- to be a pirate and Sail The Seas So I can find buried treasure and Give it to homeless people.
- that my Speech was evenbetter.

Kieran Gauci 11

I wish

I wish that my Mum won the Lottery.
She would buy me a Jeep so I
could drive adout in it
Jamie Rich age 7.

I wish

I wish that I had a really big house
and I wish that me and my mum had lot's
and lots.of money then me and my mum will
be happy.

by Melissa morden
age 8

I Wish

I Wish I had Billy back. Becausa I loved him and Lance loved him too. Mum Dad and Vikki loved him as much as I loved him. He could do a psey horn He made me laugh I wish Billy was back

By Katy Fawcett age 7

I Wish

I wish that I was a white. Power-Ranger so I could save people. Then I would be a, Hero. Then everyone would think I'am Strong and brave. That's what I wish for.

by Mitchell Cramley

I wish that
I was Who wants
to be a Millionaire
and get all the
questians right.

age 8
Natasha Bingham.

I Wish by Sarah Murphy

I wish I had lots of golden cups.
I wish the bright sun belonged to me.
I wish the snowflackes would drop on me.
I wish the world was sunny and bright.
I wish I could go in a cave with bears.
I wish winter could be more sunny.
I wish birds could allways sing to me.
I wish I could have lots of jewellery.

Iw isn

Iwish I wasa super hero. Iwish I wasapuppy. Iwish Icoulds ave peoque.

Jacqueline

age 6

I wesh

Iwish I wasasupero.

Iwould save peopple.

Leighton aged 6.

I wish

I wish I could go out to play on my motorbike.

Foster Allison
age 6

I wish

I wish I could go on holiday with my swimming costume on. I wish all my frends were like me. I wish it was Christmas every day and it was my birthday every day too. I wish I was god because I could be holy. I wish there was a fair every day. I wish it was sunny every day.

Paige Oddy aged 6

I Wish

I wish I had a meeorBike.

I would go over fields.

James aged 6

Nursery

A tortoise.

Joey Fu. Aged 4.

My goldfish

Lewis Davies. Aged 3

My
Mummy

Taylor
Thompson
Aged 3

Mrs.
Willday.

Lacey Bourne.
Aged 4.

Mrs. Willday

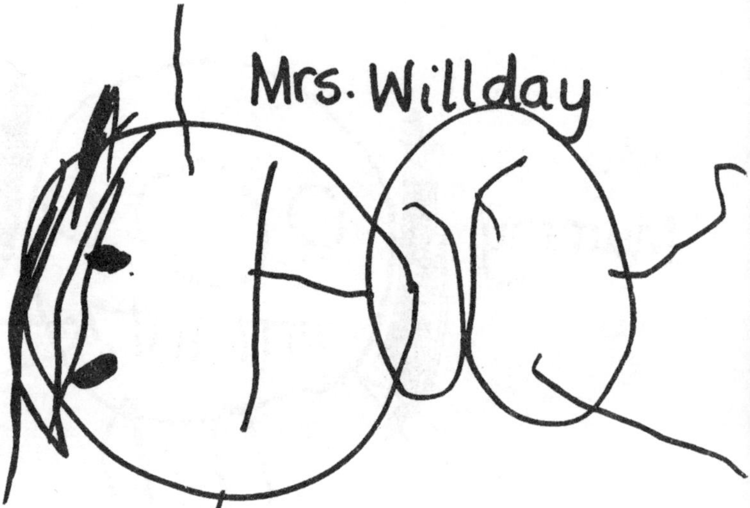

Fallon Moffat Aged 4

It's Barbie.

Charley Oulton. Aged 4.

Me and Mummy.

Jessica Ball
Aged 3

It's Po.

Lucy Rowstron.
Aged 4.

Charlie Paxton. Aged 4.

Jodie Glass. Aged 4.

Connor Deeming
and Jordan
my goldfish

Ross Moore. Aged 4.

That's my
Barbie.

Billie Walker.
Aged 3.

That's Superman.

Aidan Smith. Aged 3.

Spice my cat.

Thomas Willday. Aged 3.

Mrs. Willday.

Shaun Jellis.
Aged 4.

A teletubby.

Ema-Leigh Bourne. Aged 3.

Superman.

Luke Rowstron. Aged 4.

Jade Fallan.
Aged 3

It's Po.

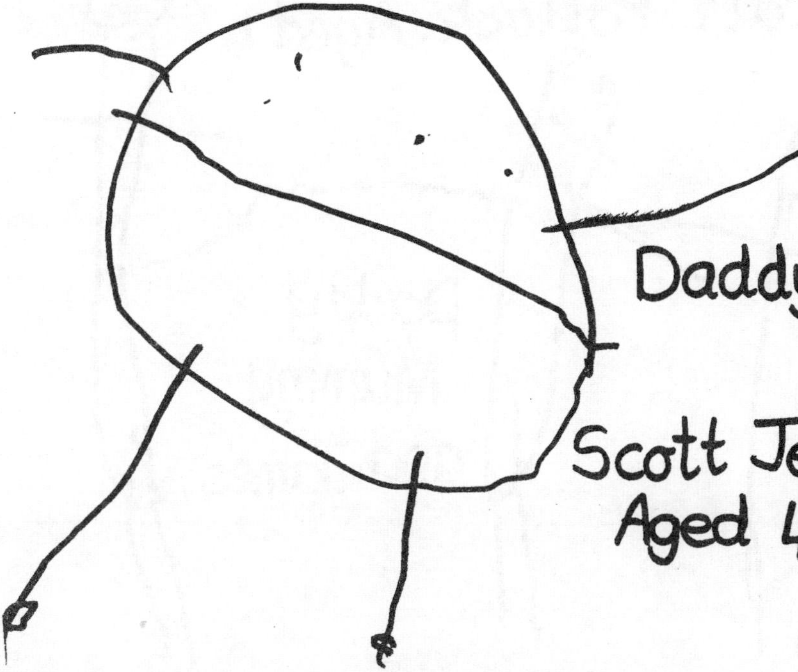

Daddy.

Scott Jellis.
Aged 4.

Mummy.

Tommy-Lee
Black.
Aged 3.

Scott Pollock. Aged 4.

Daddy, Mummy and James.

A teletubby.

Ross Cardill. Aged 3.

It's Superman.

Liam Higgins
Aged 4.

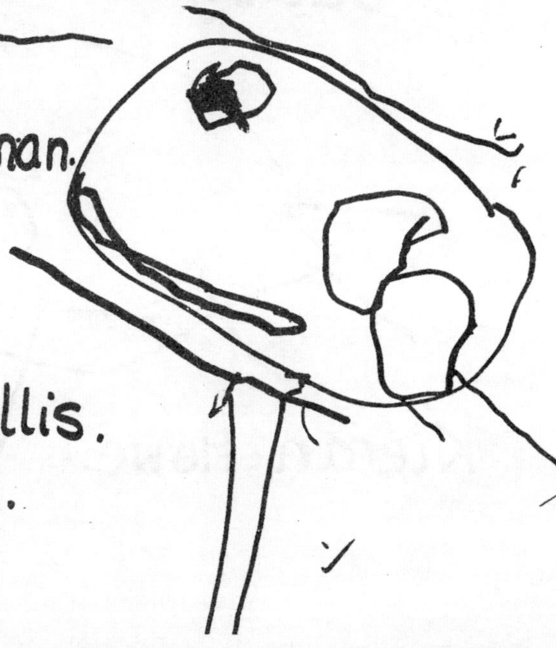

It's Superman.

Elliot Jellis.
Aged 4.

My Mummy.

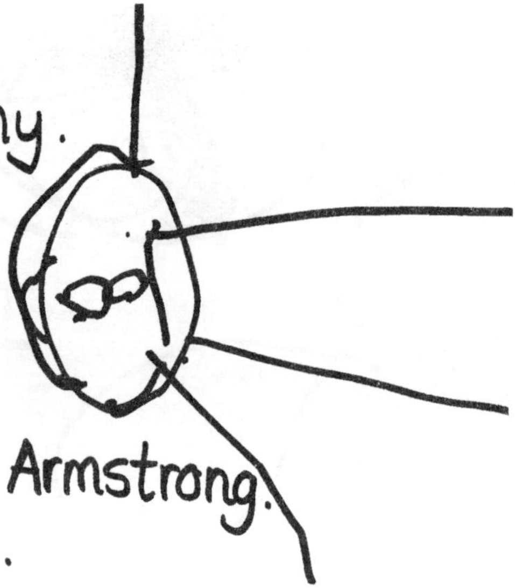

Scarlett Armstrong.
Aged 3.

Daddy.

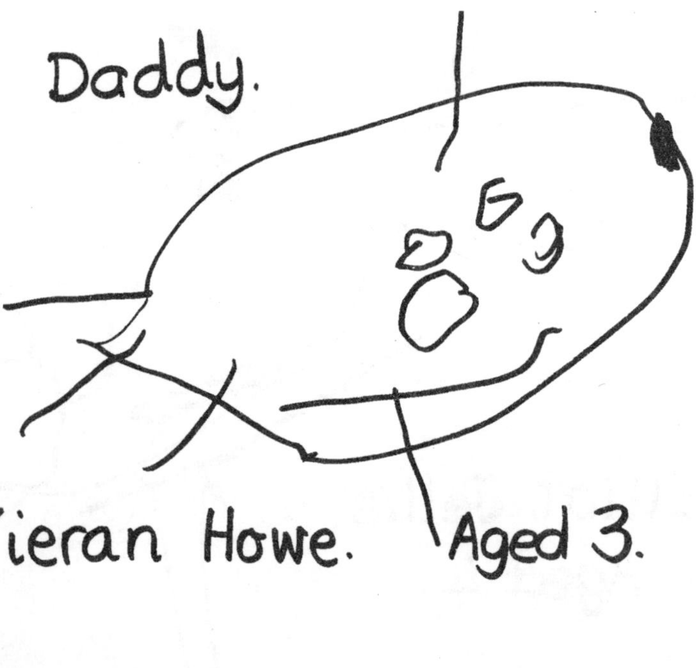

Kieran Howe. Aged 3.

Batman

Antony Richards. Aged 3.

Mrs. Cooke.

Adrian Clee. Aged 4.